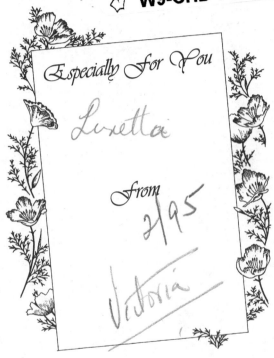

Especially For You

Luxetta

From

2/95

Victoria

To Treasure Forever

**Inspirational Poetry by
Helen Steiner Rice**

Published by:
The Robert E. and Betty P. Hopper Foundation
50 Heritage Drive
Lake Wylie, SC 29710
Phone: (803) 831-1813
Fax: (803) 831-1562

Printed in the USA

ISBN 1-56526-005-8

Stock number 00135

Foreword

Show me the way,
    not to fortune and fame,
Not how to win laurels
    or praise for my name.
But Show Me The Way
    to spread "The Great Story"
That "Thine is The Kingdom
        and Power and Glory."

Helen Steiner Rice

Contents

7

To Treasure Forever

A book for all ages,
   especially youth,
A pattern for living
   for all seekers of truth,
Words to remember
   and follow each day,
Guideposts to show you
   the safe and sure way
"To Treasure Forever,"
   as long as you live.
A real gift of love
   to keep and to give!

What Is Life?

Life is a sojourn here on earth
Which begins the day God
gives us birth,
We enter this world
from the Great Unknown
And God gives each Spirit
a form of its own
And endows this form
with a heart and a soul
To spur man on to his ultimate goal.

And through the senses
of feeling and seeing,
God makes man into a human being
So he may experience a mortal life
And through this period
of smiles and strife
Prepare himself to Return as he Came,
For birth and death
are in essence the same,
For both are fashioned
by God's mighty hand
And, while we cannot understand,
We know we are born to die and arise
For beyond this world in beauty lies
The purpose of living
and the ultimate goal
God gives at birth to each seeking soul.

So enjoy your sojourn on earth
and be glad
That God gives you a Choice
between Good Things and Bad,
And only be sure that you
Heed God's Voice
Whenever life asks you
to make a choice.

He Loves You

It's amazing and incredible,
But it's as true as it can be,
God loves and understands us all
And that means You and Me.

His grace is all sufficient
For both the Young and Old,
For the lonely and the timid,
For the brash and for the bold.

His love knows no exceptions,
So never feel excluded,
No matter Who or What you are
Your name has been included.

And no matter what your past has been,
Trust God to understand,
And no matter what your problem is
Just place it in His Hand.

For in all of our Unloveliness
This Great God Loves Us Still,
He loved us since
the world began
And what's 's more,
He Always will!

15

What Does God Know

Of These Modern Days

He sent His son to live on earth
And to walk with sinful men,
And the problems that confront us
Are the same Today as Then,
For vice and crime and evil
Prevailed in Rome and Greece
And power-driven demagogues
Incited war, not peace.

There was violence and dissension
And injustice in high courts,
And slayings were accepted
As one of the favorite sports.

Depraved, debauched and dissolute,
Men lusted after
pleasure,
They knew no god
but Power
And Gold was
their only
treasure.

So all the things we face today
Are certainly not new
And the Son of God experienced
Everything We're Going Through.

So let no one mislead you
With that hackneyed little phrase
That there's a "many-century gap"
Between God and Modern Days.

For God has seen a lot of worlds
In this same tragic state
And He knows that we are headed for
The same. grim, terrible fate
Unless man is awakened
Before the hour's too late
And at long last real-
izes
That God's Always
Up-To-Date!

A Prayer For The Young And Lovely

Dear God, I keep praying
   For the things I desire,
You tell me I'm selfish
   And "playing with fire."

It is hard to believe
   I am selfish and vain,
My desires seem so real
   And my needs seem so sane,
And yet You are wiser
   And Your vision is wide
And You look down on me
   And You see deep inside,
You know it's so easy
   To change and distort,
And things that are evil
   Seem so harmless a sport.

Oh, teach me, dear God,
    To not rush ahead
But to pray for Your guidance
    And to trust You instead,
For You know what, I need
    And that I'm only a slave
To the things that I want
    And desire and crave.

Oh, God, in Your mercy
    Look down on me now
And see in my heart
    That I love You somehow,
Although in my rashness,
    Impatience and greed
I pray for the things
    That I Want and Don't Need.

And instead of a Crown
  Please send me a Cross
And teach me to know
  That All Gain is but Loss,
And show me the way
  To joy without end,
With You as my Father,
  Redeemer and Friend
And send me the things
  That are hardest to bear,
And keep me forever
  Safe in Thy care.

New Concepts And Old Commandments

Living as we do today
 in a world of speed and greed,
We are restless and dissatisfied
 and we recognize a need
For something to alleviate
 our constant state of stress,
Something that will change dull days
 to hours of happiness,
Something new and different
 to excite our bored existence
Which we so foolishly attempt
 to change with rash resistance
By protesting we're entitled
 to the carnal-minded things,
Believing we'll be satisfied
 with the pleasure this life brings.

And in our discontentment
  we disregard restrictions
And decide to seek our happiness
  in delinquent derelictions.

We renounce our morals and ethics
  and reject all discipline,
Forgetting The Commandments
  governing now outmoded sin.

We are sure in our new freedom,
  with our lust and greed unleashed,
The "Pinnacle of Pleasure"
  will certainly be reached.

But man cannot desecrate his soul
  or defy God's changeless laws
For the age-old Ten Commandments
  Stand Untouched By Human Flaws,
And until man comes to realize
  he must live and still obey
The Commandments that God handed
  down way back in Moses' day,

He will never find contentment
  and his search will be in vain.
For what he thought was pleasure
  will return to him in pain.

For man with all his greatness,
  his knowledge and his skill,
Is still as helpless as a child
  and subject to God's will.
And there is nothing man can do
  to bring lasting joy and peace
Or curb his untamed passions
  or make his longings cease,
But the humble, full acknowledgment
  that there is no substitute
To bring forth a "Happy Harvest"
  except the "Spirit's Fruit."

For unless man's spirit is redeemed
  he will never, never find
Unblemished love and happiness
  and eternal peace of mind.

What Is Love?

*W*hat is love?
No words can define it,
It's something so great
Only God could design it …
Wonder of Wonders,
Beyond man's conception,
And only in Cod
Can love find true perfection,
For love means much more
Than small words can express,
For what man calls love
Is so very much less
Than the beauty and depth
And the true richness of
God's gift to mankind.

His compassionate love …
For love has become
A word that's misused,
Perverted, distorted
And often abused,
To speak of "light romance "
Or some affinity for
A passing attraction
That is seldom much more
Than a mere interlude
Of inflamed fascination,
A romantic fling
Of no lasting duration …
But love is enduring
And patient and kind,
It judges all things
With the heart not the mind,
And love can transform
The most common place
Into beauty and splendor
And sweetness and grace …

For love is unselfish,
Giving more than it takes,
And no matter what happens
Love never forsakes,
It's faithful and trusting
And always believing,
Guileless and honest
And never deceiving ...
Yes, love is beyond
What man can define,
For love is
Immortal
And God's Gift is
Divine.

What Is Marriage

$\mathcal{M}$arriage is the union
of two people in love,
And love is sheer magic
for it's woven of
Gossamer dreams,
enchantingly real,
That people in love
are privileged to feel.

33

But the "exquisite ecstasy"
    that captures the heart
Of two people in love
    is just a small part
Of the beauty and wonder
    and Miracle of
The growth and fulfillment
    and evolvement of love.

For only long years
    of living together
And sharing and caring
    in all kinds of weather
Both pleasure and pain,
    the glad and the sad,
Teardrops and laughter,
    the good and the bad.
Can add new dimensions
    and lift love above
The rapturous ecstasies
    of "falling in love."

For ecstasy passes
  but it is replaced
By something much greater
  that cannot be defaced.
For what was "in part"
  has now "become whole,"
For on the "wings of the flesh,"
  love entered the "Soul!"

For Girls Only

You want to be attractive
And enjoy yourself while young,
You want to be admired
And have your praises sung,
And all of this is natural
And ordained by God above
For God made man and woman
To experience Sex and Love.

But never try to prove your love
Without a wedding ring,
And never deal in "Free Love"
For There Is No Such Thing.

For "Free Love" is a
    sales pitch,
It's a game you
    cannot win,
    The best gambler
        is a loser
When you play around
        with sin.

So do not risk your chances
    For a long and happy life,
    A life of true fulfillment
That's known only to a wife.

For regardless of society
And the morals they disparage,
Nothing in the world can take
The place of Love and Marriage.

37

Worry No More God Knows The Score

*H*ave you ever been
caught
in a web you didn't weave,
Involved in conditions
that are hard to believe?
Have you felt you must speak
and explain and deny
A story that's groundless
or a small, whispered lie?
Have you ever heard rumors
you would like to refute
Or some telltale gossip
you would like to dispute?

Well, don't be upset
for God knows the score
And with God as your Judge
you need worry no more,
For men may misjudge you
but God's verdict is fair
For He looks deep inside
and He is clearly aware
Of every small detail
in your pattern of living
And always He's lenient and fair
and forgiving.

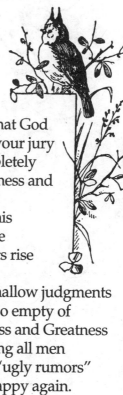

And knowing that God
is your judge and your jury
Frees you completely
from man's falseness and
fury,
And secure in this
knowledge
let your thoughts rise
above
Man's small, shallow judgments
that are so empty of
God's Goodness and Greatness
in judging all men
And forget "ugly rumors"
and be happy again.

What Is Sin?

We ask "What Is Sin"
    and how does it begin,
Does it come from Without
    or begin from Within.

Well, sin is much more
    than an Act or a Deed,
More than "false witness"
    or avarice and greed,

More than adultery
    or killing and stealing,
Sin starts with a Thought
    or an unworthy feeling
Long before it becomes
    an Act, Word or Deed,
For it grows deep within
    like a poisonous weed.

It's something we nurture
    and then cultivate
By conjuring up evils
    we then imitate,
And the longer we dwell
    on this evil within
The greater our urge
    and desire to sin,
And the less our restraint
    of unwholesome
        sensations
To deny to our bodies
    full gratifications.

And the more that we sin
    the less we detect
That in sinning we lose
    our own self-respect
And slowly we sink
    to a still lower level
Until we become merely
    "dupes of the devil,"
For sin is so subtle
    and it slips in with ease
And it gets a firm hold
    when we Do As We Please.

So ask God to help you
    to conquer desire
Aroused by the thoughts
    that have set you afire,
And remember in sinning
    there is no lasting joy
For all sin can do
    is Degrade and Destroy!

God Is The Answer

We read the headlines daily
and we listen to the news,
We are anxious and bewildered
with the world's conflicting views,
We are restless and dissatisfied
and sadly insecure,
And we voice our discontentment
over things we must endure,
For this violent age we live in
is filled with nameless fears
That grow as we discuss the things
that come daily to our ears …

So, instead of reading headlines
that disturb the heart and mind,
Let us open up the Bible
and in doing so we'll find
That this age is no different
from the millions gone before,
But in every hour of crisis
God has opened up a door
For all who sought His guidance
and trusted in His plan,
For God provides the Answer
that cannot be found by man …
And though there's hate and violence
and dissension all around,
We can always find a refuge
that is built on "solid ground"
If we go to God believing
that He hears our smallest prayer
And that nothing can befall us
when we are in His care …

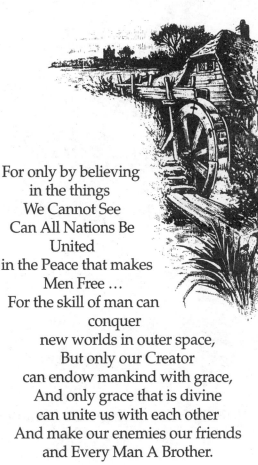

For only by believing
in the things
We Cannot See
Can All Nations Be
United
in the Peace that makes
Men Free …
For the skill of man can
conquer
new worlds in outer space,
But only our Creator
can endow mankind with grace,
And only grace that is divine
can unite us with each other
And make our enemies our friends
and Every Man A Brother.

It's A Wonderful World

In spite of the fact
we complain and
lament
And view this old world
with much discontent,
Deploring conditions
and grumbling because
There's so much injustice
and so many flaws,

It's a wonderful world
   and it's people like you
Who make it that way
   by the things that they do.

For a warm, ready smile
   or a kind, thoughtful deed,
Or a hand outstretched
   in an hour of need
Can change our whole outlook
   and make the world bright
Where a minute before
     just nothing seemed right
It's a Wonderful World
    and it always will be
If we keep our eyes open
    and focused to see
The Wonderful Things
    man is capable of
When he opens his
    heart
    to God and
    His Love.

When Troubles
Assail You,
God Will Not
Fail You

When life seems empty
And there's no place to go,
When your heart is troubled
And your spirits are low,
When friends seem few
And nobody cares
There is always God
To hear your prayers.

And whatever you're facing
Will seem much less

52

When you go to God
And confide and confess,.
For the burden that seems
Too heavy to bear
God lifts away
On the wings of prayer.

And seen through God's eyes
Earthly troubles diminish
And we're given new strength
To face and to finish
Life's daily tasks
As they come along
If we pray for strength
To keep us strong.

So go to Our Father
When troubles
assail you
For His grace is sufficient
And He'll never
fail you.

Help Yourself To Hapiness

Everybody everywhere
seeks happiness, it's true,
But finding it and keeping it
seems difficult to do,
Difficult because we think
that happiness is found
Only in the places where
wealth and fame abound.

And so we go on searching
in "palaces of pleasure"
Seeking recognition
and monetary treasure,

Unaware that happiness
   is just a "state of mind"
Within the reach of everyone
   who takes time to be kind.

For in making Others Happy
   we will be happy, too,
For the happiness you give away
   returns to "shine on you."

Not By Chance

Nor Happenstance

Into our lives come many things
to break the dull routine,
The things we had not planned on
that happen unforeseen,
The unexpected little joys
that are scattered on our way,
Success we did not count on
or a rare, fulfilling day.

A catchy, lilting melody
that makes us want to dance,
A nameless exaltation
of enchantment and romance.

An unsought word of kindness,
a compliment or two
That sets the eyes to gleaming
like crystal drops of dew.

The unplanned sudden meeting
that comes with sweet surprise
And lights the heart
with happiness
like a rainbow in the skies …

Now some folks call it fickle fate
And some folks call it chance,
While others just accept it
As a pleasant happenstance.

But no matter what you call it,
it didn't come without design,
For all our lives are fashioned
By the Hand That Is Divine.

And every happy happening
and every lucky break
Are little gifts from God above
That are ours to freely take.

Beyond Our Asking

More than hearts can imagine
    or minds comprehend,
God's bountiful gifts
    are ours without end.

We ask for a cupful
    when the vast sea is ours,
We pick a small rosebud
    from a garden of flowers,

61

We reach for a sunbeam
          but the sun still abides,
We draw one short breath
          but there's air on all sides.

Whatever we ask for
          falls short of God's giving
For His Greatness exceeds
          every facet of living,
And always God's ready
          and eager and willing
To pour out His mercy
          completely fulfilling
All of man's needs
          for peace, joy and rest
For God gives His children
          Whatever Is Best.

Just give Him a chance
    to open His Treasures
And He'll fill your life
    with unfathomable
    pleasures,
Pleasures that never
    grow worn out and
    faded
And leave us depleted,
    disillusioned and jaded.

For God has a "storehouse"
    just filled to the brim
With all that man needs
    if we'll only ask Him.

Yesterday . . . Today . . . And Tomorrow!

Yesterday's dead,
Tomorrow's unborn,
So there's nothing to fear
And nothing to mourn,
For all that is past
And all that has been
Can never return
To be lived once again.

And what lies ahead
Or the things that will be
Are still in God's Hands
So it is not up to me
To live in the future
That is God's
great unknown,
For the past and
the present

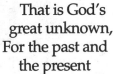

God claims for His own,
So all I need do
Is to live for Today
And trust God to show me
The Truth and
The Way.

For it's only the memory
Of things that have been
And expecting tomorrow
To bring trouble again
That fills my today,
Which God wants to bless,
With uncertain fears
And borrowed distress.

For all I need live for
Is this one little minute,
For life's Here and Now
And Eternity's in it.

Dark Shadows
Fall
In The Lives
Of Us All

Sickness and sorrow
   come to us all,
But through it we grow
   and learn to "stand tall."

For trouble is "part
   and parcel of life"
And no man can grow
   without struggle and strife,

And the more we endure
    with patience and grace
The stronger we grow
    and the more we can face.

And the more we can face,
    the greater our love,
And with love in our hearts
    we are more conscious of
The pain and the sorrow
    in lives everywhere,
So it is through trouble
    that we learn
      how to share.

Look On The Sunny Side

There are always two sides,
   the Good and the Bad,
The Dark and the Light,
   the Sad and the Glad.

But in looking back over
   the Good and the Bad
We're aware of the number
   of Good Things we've
      had.

And in counting our
   blessings
we find when we're through
We've no reason at all
   to complain or be blue.

So thank God for Good things
    He has already done,
And be grateful to Him
    for the battles you've won,
And know that the same God
    who helped you before
Is ready and willing
    to help you once more.

Then with faith in your heart
    reach out for God's Hand
And accept what He sends,
    though you can't understand.

For Our Father in heaven
    always knows what is best,
And if you trust in His wisdom
    your life will be blest,
For always remember
    that whatever betide you,
You are never alone
    for God is beside you.

The World Would Be
A Nicer Place
If We Traveled
At A
Slower Pace

Amid stresses and strains
much too many to mention,
And pressure-packed days
filled with turmoil and tension,
We seldom have time
to be "Friendly or Kind"
For we're harassed and hurried
and always behind.

72

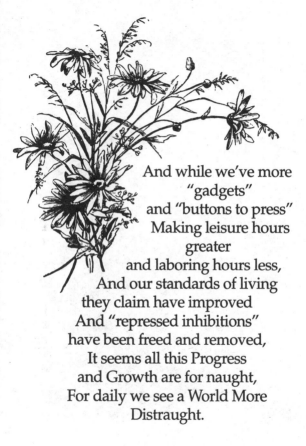

And while we've more
"gadgets"
and "buttons to press"
Making leisure hours
greater
and laboring hours less,
And our standards of living
they claim have improved
And "repressed inhibitions"
have been freed and removed,
It seems all this Progress
and Growth are for naught,
For daily we see a World More
Distraught.

74

So what does it matter
if man reaches his goal
"And gains the whole world
but loses his soul."
For what have we won
if in gaining this end
We've been much too busy
to be Kind To A Friend,
And what is there left
to make the heart sing
When life is a Cold and
Mechanical Thing
And we are but puppets
of controlled automation
Instead of "joint heirs"
to "God's Gift Of Creation."

Quit Supposin'

Don't start your day by supposin'
that trouble is just ahead,
It's better to stop supposin'
and start with a prayer instead,
And make it a prayer of Thanksgiving
for the wonderful things
God has wrought
Like the beautiful sunrise and sunset,
"God's Gifts" that are free
and not bought.

For what is the use of
supposin'
the dire things
that could happen to you
And worry about some
misfortune
that seldom if ever comes true.

But instead of just idle supposin'
step forward to meet each new day
Secure in the knowledge
God's near you
to lead you each step of the way.

For supposin'
the worst things will happen
only helps to make them come true
And you darken the bright,
happy moments
that the dear Lord has given to you.

So if you desire to be happy
and get rid of
the" Misery of Dread"
Just give up
"Supposin' The Worst
Things"
and look for
"The Best Things"
instead.

3/93

Never Borrow
Sorrow
from Tomorrow

*D*eal only with the present,
Never step into tomorrow,
For God asks us
just to trust Him
And to never borrow sorrow.

For the future is
not ours to know
And it may never be,
So let us live
and give our best
And give it lavishly.

For to meet tomorrow's troubles
Before they are even ours
Is to anticipate the Saviour
And to doubt His
all-wise powers.

So let us be content to solve
Our problems one by one,
Asking nothing of tomorrow
Except "Thy Will Be Done."

Ideals
Are
Like
Stars

In this world of casual carelessness
it's discouraging to try
To keep our morals and standards
and our Ideals High …
We are ridiculed and laughed at
by the smart sophisticate
Who proclaims in brittle banter
that such things are out of date …
But no life is worth the living
unless it's built on truth,
And we lay our life's foundation
in the golden years of youth …
So allow no one to stop you

or hinder you from laying
A firm and strong foundation
made of Faith and Love and Praying ...
And remember that Ideals
are like Stars Up In The Sky,
You can never really reach
them,
hanging in the
heavens high ...

But like the mighty mariner
who sailed the storm-tossed sea,
And used The Stars To Chart His Course
with skill and certainty,
You too can Chart Your Course In Life
with High Ideals and Love,
For High Ideals are like the Stars
that light the sky above …
You cannot ever reach them,
but Lift Your Heart Up High
And your Life Will Be As Shining
as the Stars Up In The Sky.

It Takes The Bitter
And The Sweet
To Make A Life
Full And Complete

Life is a mixture
of sunshine and rain,
Laughter and teardrops,
pleasure and pain.

Low tides and high tides,
mountains and plains,
Triumphs, defeats
and losses and gains.

But Always in All Ways
God's guiding and leading
And He alone knows
the things we're most needing.

And when He sends sorrow
or some dreaded affliction,
Be assured that it comes
with God's kind benediction.

And if we accept it
as a Gift Of His Love,
We'll be showered with blessings
from Our Father Above.

Blessings Come In Many Guises

When troubles come
  and things go wrong,
And days are cheerless
  and nights are long,
We find it so easy
  to give in to despair
By magnifying
  the burdens we bear.

We add to our worries
  by refusing to try
To look for "the rainbow"
  in an overcast sky.

And the blessing God sent
   in a "darkened disguise"
Our troubled hearts
   fail to recognize,
Not knowing God sent it
   not to distress us
But to strengthen
   our faith
   and redeem
   us and
   bless us.

A Sure Way To A Happy Day

Happiness is something
we create in our mind,
It's not something you search for
and so seldom find.
It's just waking up
and beginning the day
By counting our blessings
and kneeling to pray.

90

It's giving up thoughts
that breed discontent
And accepting what
comes
as a "gift heaven-sent."
It's giving up wishing
for things we have not
And making the best
of whatever we've got.
It's knowing that life
is determined for us,
And pursuing our tasks
without fret, fume or fuss.
For it's by completing
what God gives us to do
That we find real contentment
and happiness, too.

Conclusion

And now that you've come
to the end of the book,
Pause and reflect
and take a swift backward look
And you'll find that to follow
God's Commandments each day
Is not only the "Righteous"
and "Straight, Narrow Way"
But a Joyous Experience
for there's many a "Thrill"
In "Going God's Way"
and in Doing
His Will,

For in traveling God's Way
you are never alone
For all of your problems
God takes as His own,
And always He's ready
to counsel and guide you
And in sadness or gladness
He is always beside you,
And to live for God's glory
and to walk in His Truth
Brings peace to the aged
and joy to the youth.

And at the end of Life's Journey
there's His promised
reward
Of Life Everlasting
In The House
Of The Lord.

HELEN
STEINER
RICE